D0239616

Piano, Voice and Guitar

Arranged by Barrie Carson Turner

Best of Children's Songs

40 Well-Known Songs
in Easy Arrangements for
Piano, Voice and Guitar

ED 12948
ISMN M-2201-2546-1
ISBN 978-1-902455-83-9

SCHOTT

www.schott-music.com

Mainz · London · Madrid · New York · Paris · Prague · To'   ronto
© 2007 SCHOTT MUSIC Ltd, Londo   ny

£12·99

ED 12948

British Library Cataloguing-in-Publication Data.
A catalogue record for this book is available from the British Library
ISMN M-2201-2546-1
ISBN 978-1-902455-83-9

Design and typesetting by www.adamhaystudio.com
Music setting by Enigma Music Production Services
Printed in Germany S&Co.8193

Contents

1. Aiken Drum — 4
2. Click Go the Shears — 6
3. Donkey Riding — 8
4. A Froggy Went A-Courting — 10
5. If You're Happy and You Know It — 12
6. London Bridge is Falling Down — 14
7. Michael Finnigan — 16
8. Oh, Susanna — 18
9. Old MacDonald Had a Farm — 20
10. One More River * — 22
11. One, Two, Three, Four, Five * — 24
12. Sing a Song of Sixpence — 26
13. I Had a Little Nut Tree — 28
14. Ten in the Bed — 30
15. There's a Big Ship Sailing — 32
16. This Old Man — 34
17. Michael, Row the Boat Ashore — 36
18. She'll Be Coming Round the Mountain — 38
19. Aunt Rhody — 40
20. Bill Groggin's Goat — 42
21. Clementine — 44
22. Daisy Bell — 46
23. Down in Demerara* — 50
24. Skip to My Lou — 52
25. Ten Green Bottles — 54
26. The Grand Old Duke of York * — 56
27. There's a Hole in My Bucket — 58
28. The Green Grass Grew All Round — 60
29. The Tailor and the Mouse * — 62
30. Do Your Ears Hang Low? — 64
31. The Bear Went Over the Mountain * — 66
32. Daddy Wouldn't Buy Me a Bow-Wow — 69
33. I Had a Rooster * — 72
34. Old King Cole * — 74
35. One Man Went to Mow — 76
36. The Fox — 78
37. Yankee Doodle — 80
38. Lavender's Blue — 82
39. Kum Ba Yah — 84
40. The Old Grey Mare * — 86

(handwritten note next to item 27: I want to learn that one.)

Arranger's note: Where songs have several verses, it is likely that there may be some words or phrases that do not fit the regular pattern of syllables as set out in verse 1. The rhythm of the vocal parts should therefore be adjusted accordingly.
* Additional verses written, or words adapted, by Barrie Carson Turner.

1. Aiken Drum

Traditional
Arr. Barrie Carson Turner

2. And his hat was made of good cream cheese,
good cream cheese, good cream cheese,
And his hat was made of good cream cheese,
And his name was Aiken Drum.

And he played upon a ladle, a ladle, a ladle,
And he played upon a ladle,
And his name was Aiken Drum.

3. And his coat was made of good roast beef,
good roast beef, good roast beef,
And his coat was made of good roast beef,
And his name was Aiken Drum.

4. And his buttons were made of penny loaves,
penny loaves, penny loaves,
And his buttons were made of penny loaves,
And his name was Aiken Drum.

5. And his waistcoat was made of crust of pies,
crust of pies, crust of pies,
And his waistcoat was made of crust of pies,
And his name was Aiken Drum.

2. Click Go the Shears

Traditional
Arr. Barrie Carson Turner

With a swing

1. Down by the pen, there the old shear - er stands, Grasp - ing the shears_ in his thin bo - ny hands. Fixed is his gaze on the next sheep to come, In a lit - tle min - ute, boys, a - no - ther's done.__ *Click go the shears, boys, click, click, click.*

Wide is his blow and his hands move so quick. The ring-er looks a-round and is beat-en by a blow, Zip! A-no-ther sheep is done, and let him go. let him go.

2. Out on the floor in his cane-bottomed chair,
   There sits the boss with his eyes everywhere,
   Notes well each fleece as it comes to the screen,
   Paying strict attention that it's taken off clean.

   Click go the shears, boys, click, click, click.
   Wide is his blow and his hands move so quick.
   The ringer looks around and is beaten by a blow,
   Zip! Another sheep is done, and let him go.

3. There is the tar boy awaiting command
   With his black tar pot and his black tarry hands.
   Sees one old sheep with a cut on its back.
   Here is what he's waiting for, it's 'Tar here, Jack!'

4. Shearing is all over and we've all got our cheques,
   Roll up your swag for we're off on the tracks.
   The first pub we come to it's there we'll have a spree,
   And everyone that comes along it's 'Come and drink with me!'

screen – *the table where the wool was assessed for quality*
ringer – *a bell marked the start and end of a session*
tar boy – *any cuts to the sheep were covered with tar to seal them*

3. Donkey Riding

Traditional
Arr. Barrie Carson Turner

1. Were you ev - er in Que - bec, Stow - ing car - go on the deck,

Where there's a king with a gold - en crown Rid - ing on a don - key?

Hey, ho, a - way we go Don - key rid - ing, don - key rid - ing;

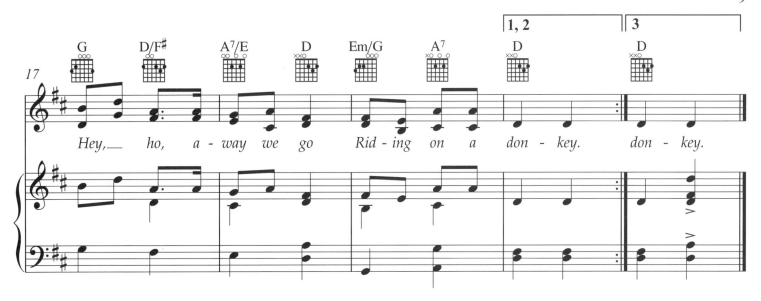

Hey,— ho, a - way we go Rid - ing on a don - key. don - key.

2. Were you ever off Cape Horn
   Where it's always fine and warm,
   And seen the lion and the unicorn
   Riding on a donkey?

   Hey, ho, away we go
   Donkey riding, donkey riding;
   Hey, ho, away we go
   Riding on a donkey.

3. Were you ever in Cardiff Bay
   Where the folks all shout, 'Hurray!
   Here comes John with his three years' pay
   Riding on a donkey?'

4. A Froggy Went A-Courting

Traditional
Arr. Barrie Carson Turner

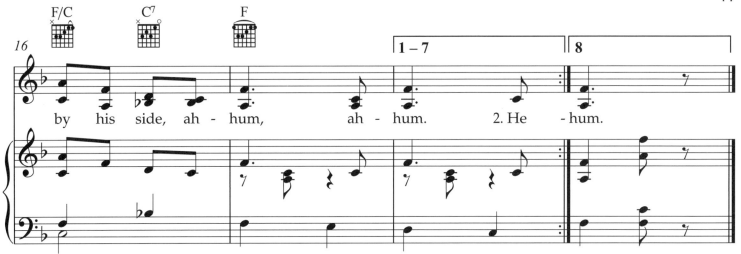

by his side, ah - hum, ah - hum. 2. He - hum.

2. He rode up to Miss Mousie's door, ah-hum, ah-hum,
   He rode up to Miss Mousie's door, ah-hum, ah-hum.
   He rode up to Miss Mousie's door
   Where he had been many times before, ah-hum, ah-hum.

3. He took Miss Mousie on his knee,
   He said, 'Miss Mouse, will you marry me?'

4. 'Without my Uncle Rat's consent
   I wouldn't marry the President'.

5. Now Uncle Rat laughed and shook his sides
   To think his niece would be a bride.

6. 'Where will the wedding breakfast be?'
   'Way down yonder in the hollow tree'.

7. They all went sailing on the lake
   And got swallowed up by a big fat snake.

8. There's bread and cheese upon the shelf,
   If you want any more you can sing it yourself.

5. If You're Happy and You Know It

Traditional
Arr. Barrie Carson Turner

hap - py and you know it, Then you'll real - ly want to show it, If you're

1 – 5 **6**

hap - py and you know it, clap your hands. *clap* *clap* 2. If you're eyes. *blink* *blink*

2. If you're happy and you know it, stamp your feet.
   If you're happy and you know it, stamp your feet.
   If you're happy and you know it,
   Then you'll surely want to show it,
   If you're happy and you know it, stamp your feet.

3. If you're happy and you know it, nod your head.

4. If you're happy and you know it, wave your hand.

5. If you're happy and you know it, shout 'Hooray'.

6. If you're happy and you know it, blink your eyes.

6. London Bridge is Falling Down

Traditional
Arr. Barrie Carson Turner

3. Build it up with silver and gold,
   Silver and gold, silver and gold.
   Build it up with silver and gold,
   My fair lady.

4. Silver and gold will be stolen away,
   Stolen away, stolen away.
   Silver and gold will be stolen away,
   My fair lady.

5. Build it up with wood and clay,
   Wood and clay, wood and clay.
   Build it up with wood and clay,
   My fair lady.

6. Wood and clay will wash away,
   Wash away, wash away.
   Wood and clay will wash away,
   My fair lady.

7. Build it up with iron and steel,
   Iron and steel, iron and steel.
   Build it up with iron and steel,
   My fair lady.

8. Iron and steel will bend and bow,
   Bend and bow, bend and bow.
   Iron and steel will bend and bow,
   My fair lady.

9. Build it up with stone so strong,
   Stone so strong, stone so strong.
   Build it up with stone so strong,
   My fair lady.

10. Stone will last for ages long,
    Ages long, ages long.
    Stone will last for ages long,
    My fair lady.

7. Michael Finnigan

Traditional
Arr. Barrie Carson Turner

was an old man called Mich - ael Finn - i - gan, He grew whisk - ers

on his chin - i - gain, The wind came up and blew them in - a - gin,

Poor old Mich - ael Finn - i - gan — be - gin a - gin....2. There Finn - i - gan.

2. There was an old man called Michael Finnigan,
He kicked up an awful dinigin
Because they said he must not singigin,
Poor old Michael Finnigan – *begin agin…*

3. There was an old man called Michael Finnigan,
He went fishing with a pinigin,
Caught a fish but dropped it inagin,
Poor old Michael Finnigan – *begin agin…*

4. There was an old man called Michael Finnigan,
Climbed a tree and barked his shinigin,
Took off several yards of skinigin,
Poor old Michael Finnigan – *begin agin…*

5. There was an old man called Michael Finnigan,
He grew fat, and then grew thinagin,
Then he died – that's the end, *can't begin agin.*
Poor old Michael Finnigan.

8. Oh, Susanna

Traditional
Arr. Barrie Carson Turner

Steadily

come from Al - a - bam - a With my ban - jo on my knee;___ I'm___

goin' to Lou' - si - an - a, My true love for to see. It___

rained all night the day I left, The weath - er it was dry,___ The___

2. I had a dream the other night
When everything was still;
I thought I saw Susanna
A-coming down the hill.
A buckwheat cake was in her mouth,
A tear was in her eye;
Says I, 'I'm comin' from the South,
Susanna, don't you cry'.

Oh, Susanna,
Oh, don't you cry for me.
I've come from Alabama
With my banjo on my knee.

Buckwheat cake – *a pancake made with flour ground from the seeds of the Asian Buckwheat plant*

9. Old MacDonald Had a Farm

Traditional
Arr. Barrie Carson Turner

2. Old MacDonald had a farm, E I E I O.
   And on that farm he had some ducks, E I E I O.
   With a quack-quack here and a quack-quack there,
   Here a quack, there a quack, everywhere a quack-quack.
   Old MacDonald had a farm, E I E I O.

3. Old MacDonald had a farm, E I E I O.
   And on that farm he had some sheep, E I E I O.
   With a baa-baa here and a baa-baa there,
   Here a baa, there a baa, everywhere a baa-baa.
   Old MacDonald had a farm, E I E I O.

4. Old MacDonald had a farm, E I E I O.
   And on that farm he had some pigs, E I E I O.
   With a grunt-grunt here and a grunt-grunt there,
   Here a grunt, there a grunt, everywhere a grunt-grunt.
   Old MacDonald had a farm, E I E I O.

This song lends itself very easily to further verses!

10. One More River

Traditional
Arr. Barrie Carson Turner

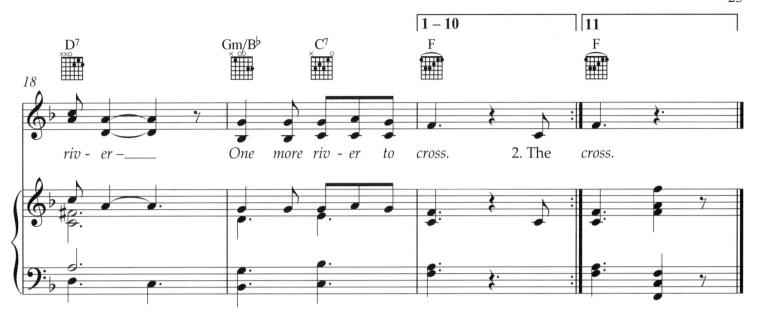

2. The animals went in one by one –
   One more river to cross.
   The elephant chewing a carraway bun –
   One more river to cross.

   One more river –
   That's the river of Jordan.
   One more river –
   One more river to cross.

3. The animals went in two by two,
   The crocodile and the kangaroo.

4. The animals went in three by three,
   The tall giraffe and the tiny flea.

5. The animals went in four by four,
   The fat hippopotamus stuck in the door.

6. The animals went in five by five,
   The bumble bee with a five-star hive.

7. The animals went in six by six,
   The monkey was up to his usual tricks.

8. The animals went in seven by seven,
   The sea slug winked at a bat called Kevin.

9. The animals went in eight by eight,
   Some eager to board just climbed the gate.

10. The animals went in nine by nine,
    The emu said, 'That front seat's mine!'

11. The animals went in ten by ten,
    Then Noah he pulled the gangway in.

11. One, Two, Three, Four, Five

Traditional
Arr. Barrie Carson Turner

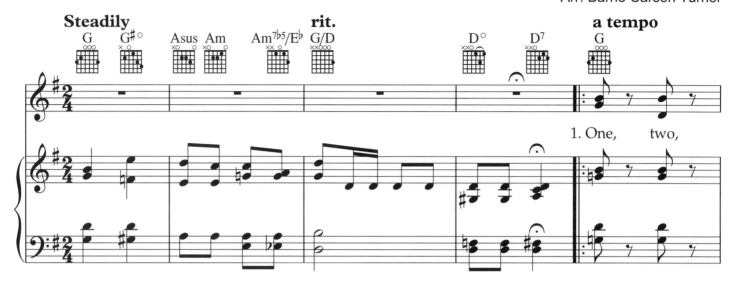

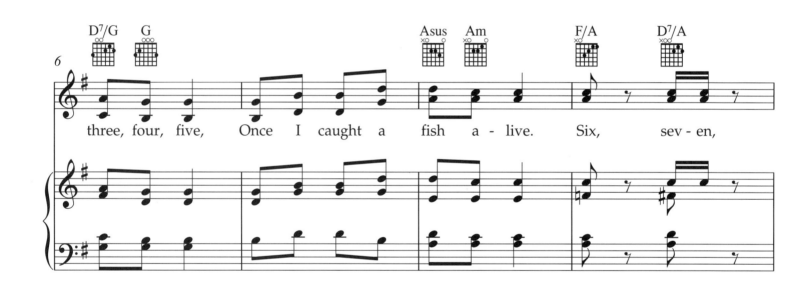

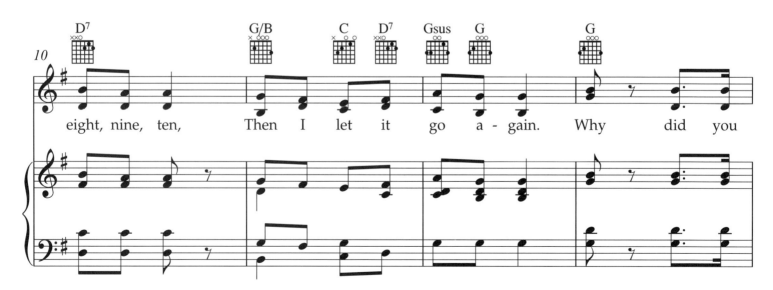

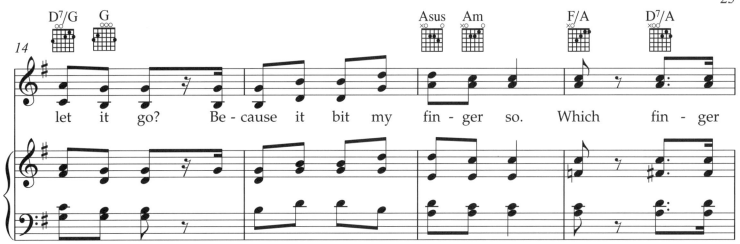

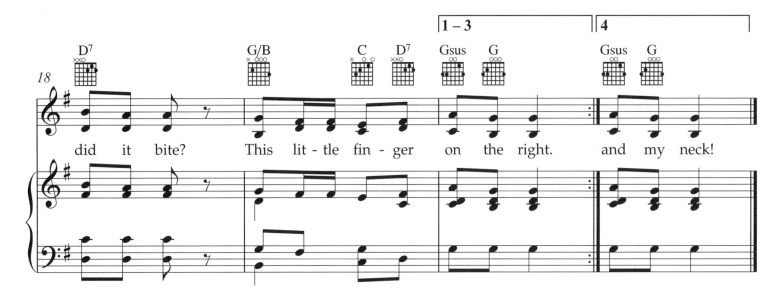

2. One, two, three, four, five,
   Once I caught a bee alive.
   Six, seven, eight, nine, ten,
   Then I let it go again.
   Why did you let it go?
   Because it stung my finger so.
   Which finger did it sting?
   This little finger, near my ring.

3. One, two, three, four, five,
   Once I caught a mouse alive.
   Six, seven, eight, nine, ten,
   Then I let it go again.
   Why did you let it go?
   Because it nipped my finger so.
   Which finger did it nip?
   This little finger, where I grip.

4. One, two, three, four, five,
   Once I caught a bird alive.
   Six, seven, eight, nine, ten,
   Then I let it go again.
   Why did you let it go?
   Because it pecked my finger so.
   Which finger did it peck?
   This little finger – *and my neck!*

12. Sing a Song of Sixpence

Traditional
Arr. Barrie Carson Turner

1. Sing a song of six-pence, A pock-et full of rye, Four and twen-ty black-birds

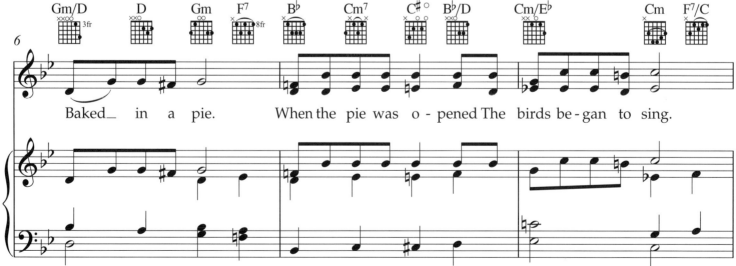

Baked__ in a pie. When the pie was o-pened The birds be-gan to sing.

Was-n't that a dain-ty dish to set be-fore the king! 2. The

pecked off her nose. D.$ (vs. 1) Set be-fore the king!

2. The king was in his counting house,
   Counting out his money.
   The queen was in the parlour,
   Eating bread and honey.
   The maid was in the garden,
   Hanging out the clothes,
   When down came a blackbird
   And pecked off her nose.

13. I Had a Little Nut Tree

Traditional
Arr. Barrie Carson Turner

1. I had a lit-tle nut tree,

No-thing would it bear, But a sil-ver nut-meg And a gol-den pear; The

King of Spain's daugh-ter Came to vis-it me, And all___ for the sake Of my

2. Her dress was made of crimson,
Jet black was her hair,
She asked me for my nut tree
And my golden pear.
I said, 'So fair a princess
Never did I see,
I'll give you all the fruit
From my little nut tree'.

I skipped over water,
I danced over sea,
And all the birds in the air
Couldn't catch me.

14. Ten in the Bed

Traditional
Arr. Barrie Carson Turner

2. There were NINE in the bed
   And the little one said...

3. There were EIGHT in the bed
   And the little one said...

4. There were SEVEN in the bed
   And the little one said...

5. There were SIX in the bed
   And the little one said...

6. There were FIVE in the bed
   And the little one said...

7. There were FOUR in the bed
   And the little one said...

8. There were THREE in the bed
   And the little one said...

9. There were TWO in the bed
   And the little one said...

10. There was ONE in the bed
    And the little one said,
    'Good night! Good night!'

15. There's a Big Ship Sailing

Traditional
Arr. Barrie Carson Turner

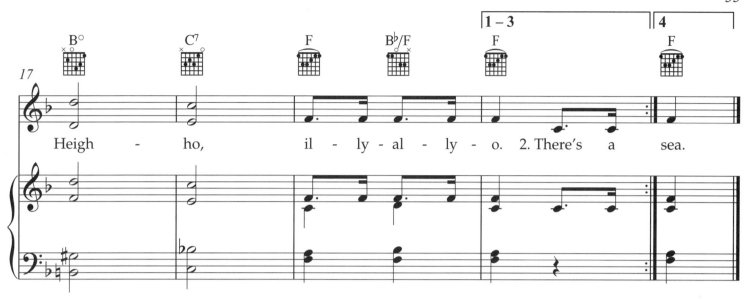

Heigh - ho, il - ly - al - ly - o. 2. There's a sea.

2. There's a big ship sailing and a-rocking on the sea,
   A-rocking on the sea, a-rocking on the sea.
   There's a big ship sailing and a-rocking on the sea,
   Heigh-ho, rocking on the sea.

3. The captain said, 'It'll never, never do,
   Never, never do, never, never do'.
   The captain said, 'It'll never, never do,
   Heigh-ho, never, never do'.

4. Oh, the big ship sank to the bottom of the sea,
   The bottom of the sea, the bottom of the sea.
   Oh, the big ship sank to the bottom of the sea,
   Heigh-ho, the bottom of the sea.

16. This Old Man

Traditional
Arr. Barrie Carson Turner

1. This old man, he played ONE, He played nick nack on my drum.

Nick nack pad-dy whack, give a dog a bone,_ This old man came rol-ling home. rol-ling home.

2. This old man, he played TWO,
   He played nick nack on my shoe.

   Nick nack paddy whack, give a dog a bone,
   This old man came rolling home.

3. This old man, he played THREE,
   He played nick nack on my tree.

4. This old man, he played FOUR,
   He played nick nack on my door.

5. This old man, he played FIVE,
   He played nick nack on my hive.

6. This old man, he played SIX,
   He played nick nack on my sticks.

7. This old man, he played SEVEN,
   He played nick nack up in heaven.

8. This old man, he played EIGHT,
   He played nick nack on my gate.

9. This old man, he played NINE,
   He played nick nack on my sign.

10. This old man, he played TEN,
    He played nick nack on my hen.

17. Michael, Row the Boat Ashore

Traditional
Arr. Barrie Carson Turner

Slow, rocking tempo

Mich - ael, row the boat a - shore, Hal - le - lu - jah. Mich - ael, row the boat a - shore, Hal - le - lu - jah.

Fine

1. Sis - ter, help to trim the sail, Hal - le - lu - jah. Sis - ter,

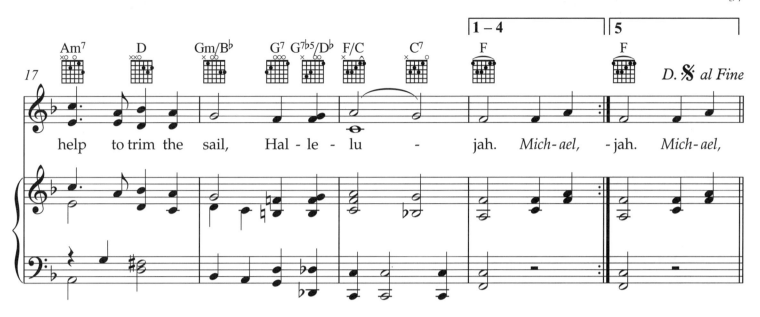

Michael, row the boat ashore, hallelujah.
Michael, row the boat ashore, hallelujah.

2. Brother, won't you lend a hand, hallelujah.
   Steer us to the promised land, hallelujah.

3. Children, sing a happy song, hallelujah.
   Help to speed the boat along, hallelujah.

4. River Jordan's deep and wide, hallelujah.
   Milk and honey on the other side, hallelujah.

5. If you get there before I do, hallelujah.
   Tell my people I'm coming too, hallelujah.

18. She'll Be Coming Round the Mountain

Traditional
Arr. Barrie Carson Turner

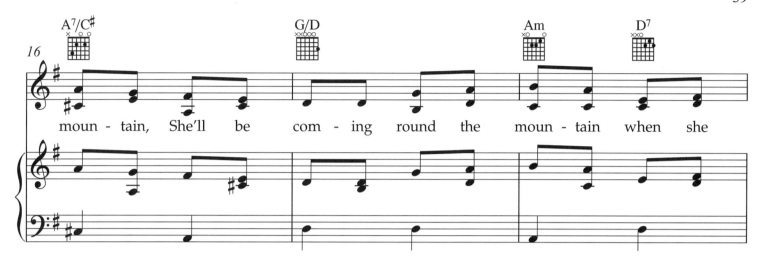

mountain, She'll be coming round the mountain when she

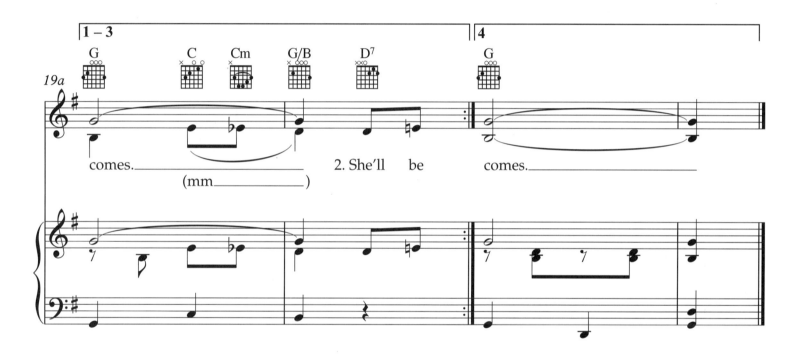

comes. _____
(mm _____)
2. She'll be comes. _____

2. She'll be driving six white horses when she comes.
   She'll be driving six white horses when she comes.
   She'll be driving six white horses,
   She'll be driving six white horses,
   She'll be driving six white horses when she comes.

3. Oh, we'll all go out to greet her when she comes.
   Oh, we'll all go out to greet her when she comes.
   Oh, we'll all go out to greet her,
   Oh, we'll all go out to greet her,
   Oh, we'll all go out to greet her when she comes.

4. And we'll all have chicken and dumplings when she comes.
   And we'll all have chicken and dumplings when she comes.
   And we'll all have chicken and dumplings,
   And we'll all have chicken and dumplings,
   And we'll all have chicken and dumplings when she comes.

19. Aunt Rhody

Traditional
Arr. Barrie Carson Turner

Moderately slow

1. Go tell Aunt Rho - dy, Go tell Aunt Rho - dy, Go tell Aunt

Rho - dy Her old grey goose is dead. 2. The dead.

2. The one she's been saving,
   The one she's been saving,
   The one she's been saving
   To make a feather bed.

3. She died in the millpond,
   She died in the millpond,
   She died in the millpond
   A-standin' on her head.

4. The old gander's mourning,
   The old gander's mourning,
   The old gander's mourning
   Because his wife is dead.

5. The goslings are crying,
   The goslings are crying,
   The goslings are crying
   Because their mother's dead.

6. Go tell Aunt Rhody,
   Go tell Aunt Rhody,
   Go tell Aunt Rhody
   Her old grey goose is dead.

20. Bill Groggin's Goat

Traditional
Arr. Barrie Carson Turner

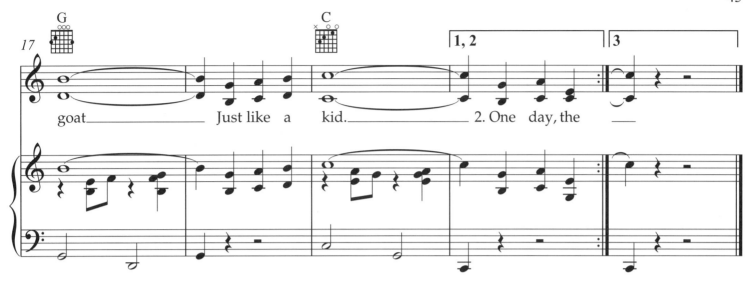

goat_____ Just like a kid._____ 2. One day, the ___

2. One day, the goat
   Felt frisk and fine,
   Ate three red shirts
   Right off the line.
   The man, he grabbed
   Him by the back
   And tied him to
   A railroad track.

3. Now, when that train
   Hove into sight,
   That goat grew pale,
   And green with fright.
   He heaved a sigh,
   As if in pain,
   Coughed up the shirts
   And flagged the train.

21. Clementine

Traditional
Arr. Barrie Carson Turner

1. In a cav - ern, in a can - yon, Ex - ca - va - ting for a mine, Dwelt a mi - ner, for - ty - ni - ner, And his daught - er Clem - en - tine.

2. Light she was, and like a fairy,
   And her shoes were number nine;
   Herring-boxes without topses,
   Sandals were for Clementine.

   Oh my darling, oh my darling, oh my darling Clementine!
   You are lost and gone for ever, dreadful sorry, Clementine.

3. Drove she ducklings to the water
   Every morning, just at nine;
   Hit her foot against a splinter,
   Fell into the foaming brine.

4. Saw her lips above the water
   Blowing bubbles mighty fine;
   But alas! I was no swimmer,
   So I lost my Clementine.

5. In a corner of the churchyard
   Where the myrtle boughs entwine,
   Grow the roses in their posies
   Fertilized by Clementine.

6. Then the miner, forty-niner,
   Soon began to peak and pine,
   Thought he oughter join his daughter –
   Now he's with his Clementine.

22. Daisy Bell

Words and Music by Harry Dacre (1860–1922)
Arr. Barrie Carson Turner

Moderate waltz

1. There is a flow-er with-in my heart, Dai -

sy, Dai - sy! Plan-ted one day by a

2. We will go 'tandem' as man and wife,
   Daisy, Daisy!
   'Pedalling' away down the road of life,
   I and my Daisy Bell!
   When the road's dark we can both despise
   Policeman and lamps as well;
   There are bright lights in the dazzling eyes
   Of beautiful Daisy Bell!

3. I will stand by you in 'wheel' or woe,
   Daisy, Daisy!
   You'll be the 'bell' which I'll ring, you know!
   Sweet little Daisy Bell!
   You'll take the lead in each trip we take,
   Then if I don't do well;
   I will permit you to use the brake,
   My beautiful Daisy Bell!

23. Down in Demerara

Traditional
Arr. Barrie Carson Turner

1. There was a man who had a hors-e-lum,

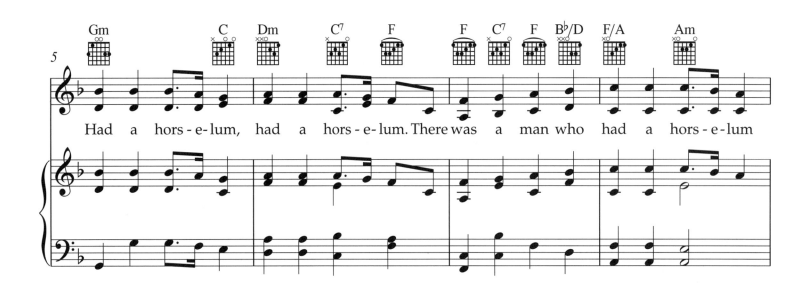

Had a hors-e-lum, had a hors-e-lum. There was a man who had a hors-e-lum

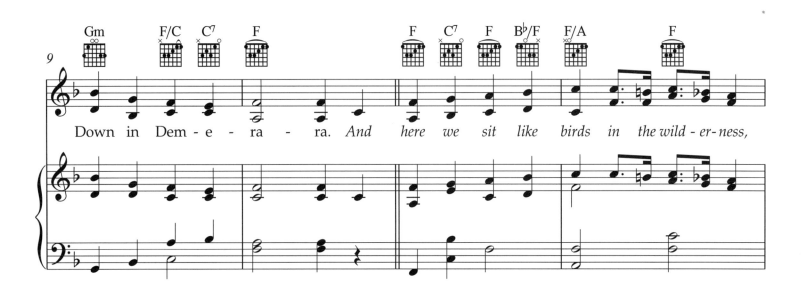

Down in Dem-e-ra-ra. *And here we sit like birds in the wild-er-ness,*

2. Now that poor horse, he broke his legalum,
   Broke his legalum, broke his legalum.
   Now that poor horse, he broke his legalum,
   Down in Demerara.

   And here we sit like birds in the wilderness,
   Birds in the wilderness, birds in the wilderness.
   Here we sit like birds in the wilderness,
   Down in Demerara.

3. Now that poor man, he sent for a doctorum.

4. The doctor said, 'It's very badalum'.

5. Now that poor horse, he went and diedalum.

6. And that is the end of this sad storyum.

24. Skip to My Lou

Traditional
Arr. Barrie Carson Turner

Skip, skip, skip to my Lou,
Skip, skip, skip to my Lou,
Skip, skip, skip to my Lou,
Skip to my Lou, my darling.

2. I'll get another one prettier than you.

3. Cows in the field go moo, moo, moo.

4. Flies in the buttermilk, shoo, fly, shoo!

5. Little red wagon is painted blue.

25. Ten Green Bottles

Traditional
Arr. Barrie Carson Turner

1. There were TEN green bot-tles hang-ing on the wall, TEN green bot-tles hang-ing on the wall, And if one green bot-tle should ac-ci-dent-'ly fall, There'd be

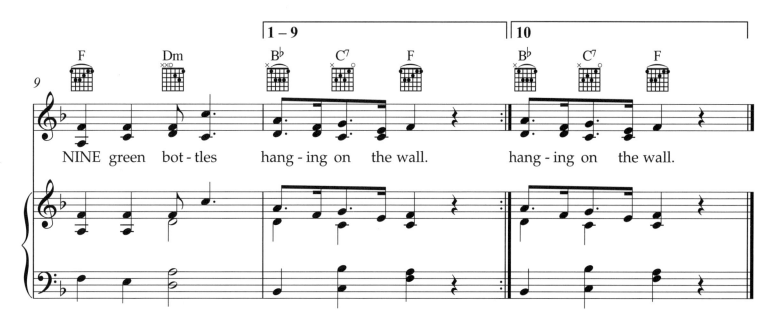

2. NINE green bottles hanging on the wall,
   NINE green bottles hanging on the wall,
   And if one green bottle should accident'ly fall,
   There'd be EIGHT green bottles hanging on the wall.

   Continue to 'TWO green bottles', then last verse:

10. There was ONE green bottle hanging on the wall,
    ONE green bottle hanging on the wall,
    And if that green bottle should accident'ly fall,
    There'd be no green bottles hanging on the wall.

26. The Grand Old Duke of York

Traditional
Arr. Barrie Carson Turner

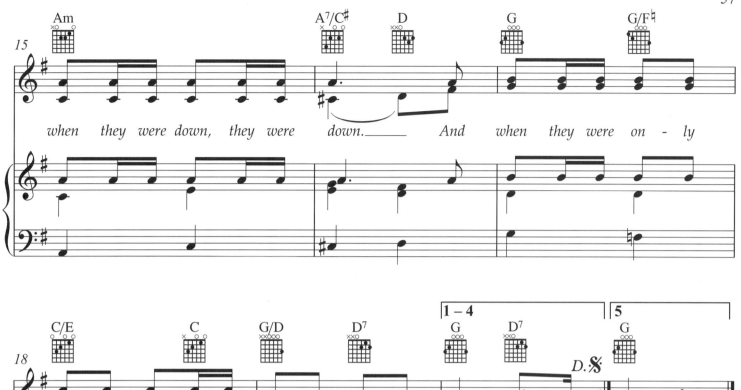

when they were down, they were down.____ And when they were on - ly

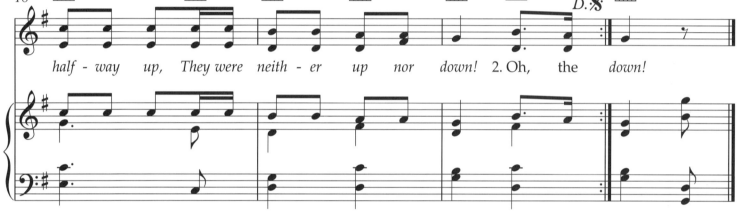

half - way up, They were neith - er up nor down! 2. Oh, the down!

2. Oh, the grand old Duke of York,
   He had ten thousand men,
   They beat their drums as they marched up the hill
   And they beat them down again.

   And when they were up, they were up.
   And when they were down, they were down.
   And when they were only half way up
   They were neither up nor down!

3. They waved their flags.

4. They raised their hats.

5. They clicked their heels.

27. There's a Hole in My Bucket

Fairly slow

Traditional
Arr. Barrie Carson Turner

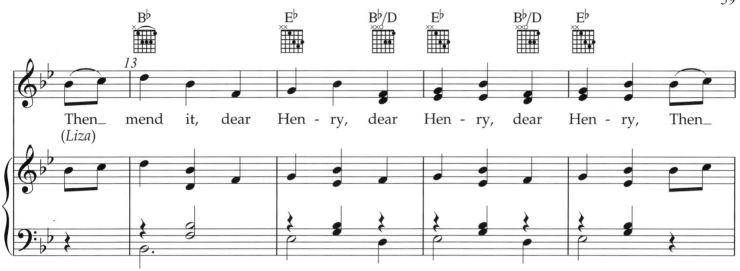

2. (*Henry*) But with what shall I mend it, dear Liza?
(*Liza*) With a straw, dear Henry.

3. But the straw is too long, dear Liza.
Then cut it, dear Henry.

4. But with what shall I cut it, dear Liza?
With a knife, dear Henry.

5. But the knife is too blunt, dear Liza.
Then sharpen it, dear Henry.

6. But with what shall I sharpen it, dear Liza?
With a stone, dear Henry.

7. But the stone is too dry, dear Liza.
Then wet it, dear Henry.

8. But with what shall I wet it, dear Liza?
With water, dear Henry.

9. But in what shall I carry it, dear Liza?
In a bucket, dear Henry.

28. The Green Grass Grew All Round

Traditional
Arr. Barrie Carson Turner

Moderately

1. In a wood there was a tree, The fin-est tree you ev-er did see, And the

tree was in the wood, *And the green grass grew a - round, a-round, a-round, And the*

Repeat as necessary

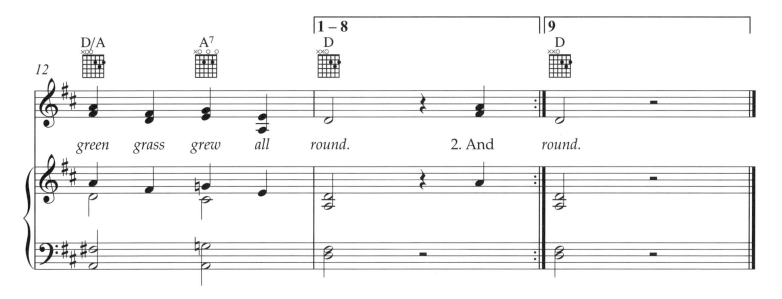

2. And on this tree there was a branch,
   The finest branch you ever did see,
   And the branch was on the tree,
   And the tree was in the wood,
   And the green grass grew around, around, around,
   And the green grass grew all round.

3. And on this branch there was a twig,
   The finest twig you ever did see,
   And the twig was on the branch,
   And the branch was on the tree,
   And the tree was in the wood,
   And the green grass grew around, around, around,
   And the green grass grew all round.

4. And on this twig there was a nest,
   And the nest was on the twig...

5. And in this nest there was a bird,
   And the bird was in the nest...

6. And on this bird there was a wing,
   And the wing was on the bird...

7. And on this wing there was a feather,
   And the feather was on the wing...

8. And on this feather there was a flea,
   And the flea was on the feather...

9. And on this flea there was a hair,
   And the hair was on the flea.

29. The Tailor and the Mouse

Traditional
Arr. Barrie Carson Turner

1. There was a tai - lor had a mouse, *Hey did - dle um - tum fee - dle.* They

lived to - ge - ther in one house, *Hey did - dle um - tum fee - dle.*

Hey did - dle um - tum, ta - rum tum tum, Through the town of Ram - sey, Hey did - dle um - tum

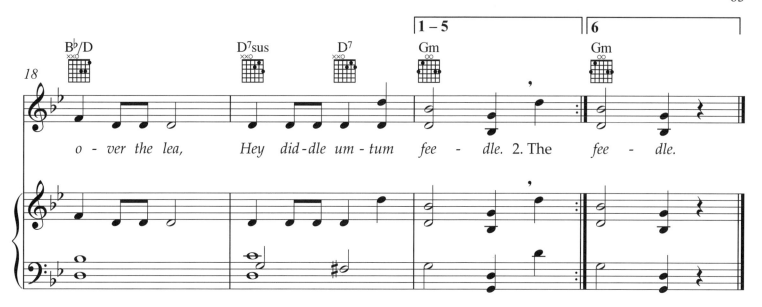

o - ver the lea,   Hey did -dle um - tum   fee - dle. 2. The   fee - dle.

2. The tailor bought a fine silk hat,
   Hey diddle um-tum feedle.
   The mouse, he ate it – just like that!
   Hey diddle um-tum feedle.

   Hey diddle um-tum, tarum tum-tum,
   Through the town of Ramsey,
   Hey diddle um-tum over the lea,
   Hey diddle um-tum feedle.

3. The hat, it was so hard to chew,
   Hey diddle um-tum feedle.
   It tasted just like year-old glue,
   Hey diddle um-tum feedle.

4. The tailor thought the mouse would die,
   Hey diddle um-tum feedle,
   A tear fell from his glistening eye.
   Hey diddle um-tum feedle.

5. The tailor saved the mouse's life,
   Hey diddle um-tum feedle.
   He fished the hat out with a knife,
   Hey diddle um-tum feedle.

6. The moral of this sad debate,
   Hey diddle um-tum feedle.
   Is seize the moment – don't be late,
   Hey diddle um-tum feedle.

30. Do Your Ears Hang Low?

Traditional
Arr. Barrie Carson Turner

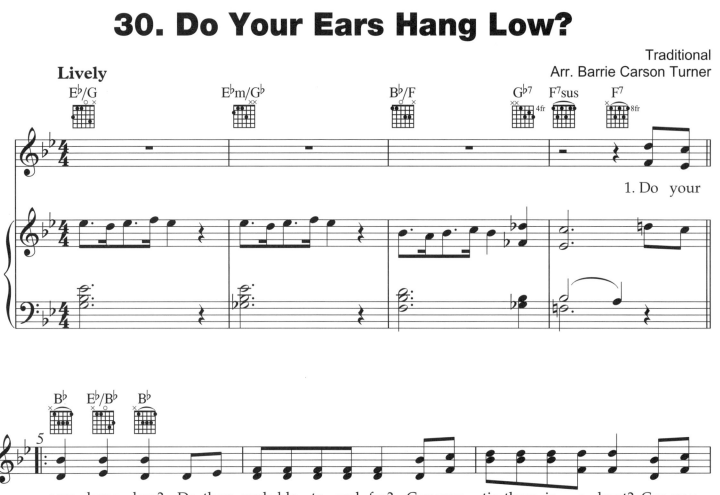

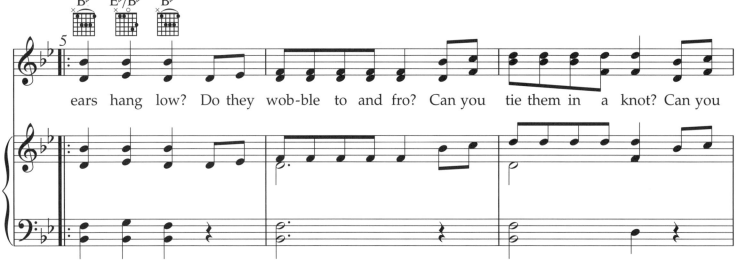

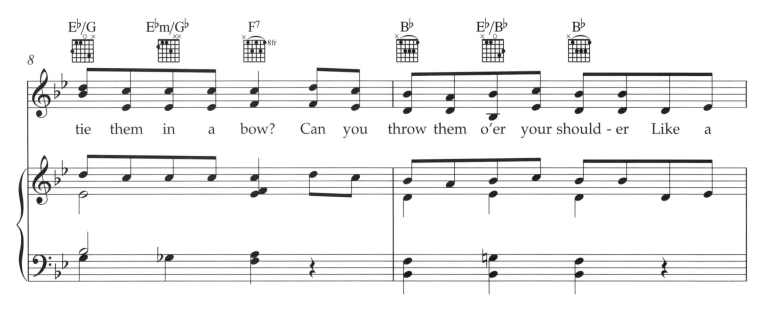

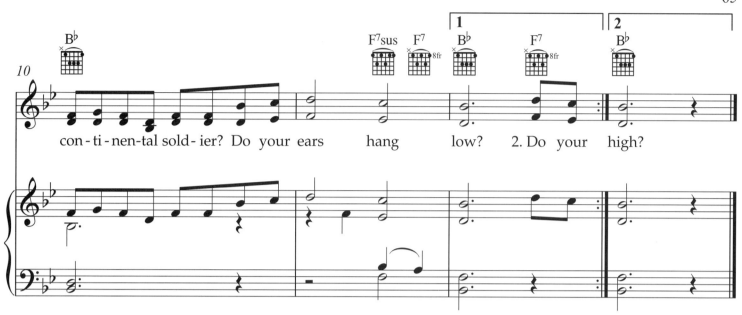

2. Do your ears stand high?
   Do they stand up to the sky?
   Can they stand up if they're wet?
   Can they stand up if they're dry?
   Can you wave them to your neighbour
   With a minimum of labour?
   Do your ears stand high?

31. The Bear Went Over the Mountain

Traditional
Arr. Barrie Carson Turner

2. Oh, the pig walked into the hen-house,
   The pig walked into the hen-house,
   The pig walked into the hen-house
   To see what he could see;
   To see what he could see,
   To see what he could see.
   Oh, the pig walked into the hen-house,
   The pig walked into the hen-house,
   The pig walked into the hen-house
   To see what he could see.
   He saw a bunch of hens,
   He saw a bunch of hens!
   Oh, the pig walked into the hen-house,
   The pig walked into the hen-house,
   The pig walked into the hen-house
   To see what he could see.

3. Oh, the bee buzzed down to the shoe store.
   He saw a load of shoes.

4. Oh, the bird swam under the ocean
   He saw a stack of fish.

32. Daddy Wouldn't Buy Me a Bow-Wow

Words and Music by Joseph Tabrar (1857–1931)
Arr. Barrie Carson Turner

bow - wow (bow - wow). I've got a lit - tle cat, I am ve - ry fond of that, But I'd

1, 3, 5   **2, 4**   **6**

ra-ther have a bow-wow, wow-wow, wow-wow.   wow.   2. We   wow.

2. We used to have two tiny dogs,
   Such pretty little dears,
   But daddy sold 'em 'cause they used
   To bite each other's ears;
   I cried all day – at eight at night
   Papa sent me to bed,
   When ma came home and wiped my eyes,
   I cried again, and said –

   Daddy wouldn't buy me a bow-wow (bow-wow),
   Daddy wouldn't buy me a bow-wow (bow-wow).
   I've got a little cat,
   I am very fond of that,
   But I'd rather have a bow-wow, wow-wow, wow-wow.
   Daddy wouldn't buy me a bow-wow (bow-wow),
   Daddy wouldn't buy me a bow-wow (bow-wow),
   I've got a little cat,
   I am very fond of that,
   But I'd rather have a bow-wow wow.

3. I'll be so glad when I get old,
   To do just as I please,
   I'll have a dozen bow-wows then,
   A parrot and some bees;
   Whene'er I see a tiny pet,
   I'll kiss the little thing,
   'Twill remind me of the time gone by,
   When I would cry and sing –

Form – long bench used for seating, especially in schools in Victorian Britain

33. I Had a Rooster

Traditional
Arr. Barrie Carson Turner

3. I had a duckling, and the duckling pleased me,
   I fed my duckling 'neath a green berry tree.
   The little duckling went, 'Quack, quack, quack'.
   The little kitten went, 'Meow, meow, meow'.
   The little rooster went, 'Cock-a-doodle-doo,
   Dee-doodle-dee, doodle-dee, doodle-dee-doo'.

4. I had a puppy... woof...

5. I had a spider... spin...

6. I had a pony... neigh...

34. Old King Cole

Traditional
Arr. Barrie Carson Turner

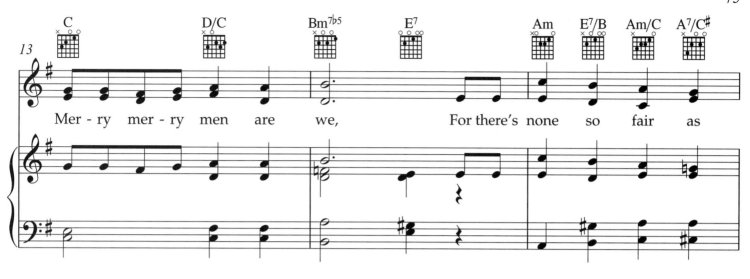

Mer - ry mer - ry men are we, For there's none so fair as

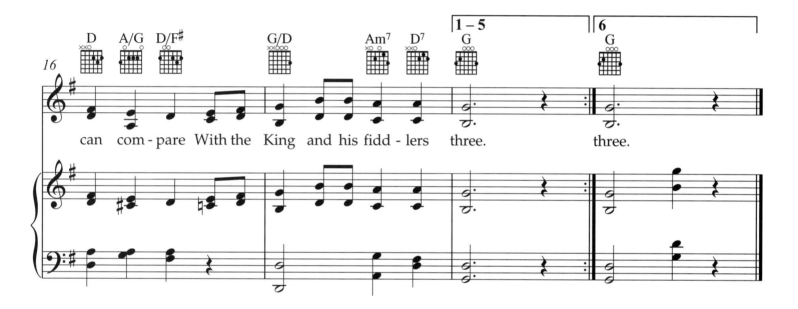

can com - pare With the King and his fidd - lers three. three.

2. Old King Cole was a merry old soul
   And a merry old soul was he.
   He called for his pipe and he called for his bowl,
   And he called for his drummers three.
   Trrum, trrum, trrum went the drummers,
   Scrape, scrape, scrape went the fiddlers,
   Merry, merry men are we,
   For there's none so fair as can compare
   With the King and his drummers three.

3. Toot, toot, toot went the flautists.

4. Traa, traa, traa went the trumpets.

5. Oo, oo, oo went the singers.

6. Umph, umph, umph went the tubas.

35. One Man Went to Mow

Traditional
Arr. Barrie Carson Turner

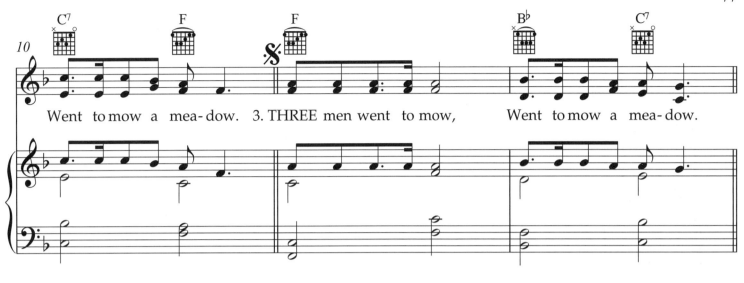

Went to mow a mea-dow. 3. THREE men went to mow, Went to mow a mea-dow.

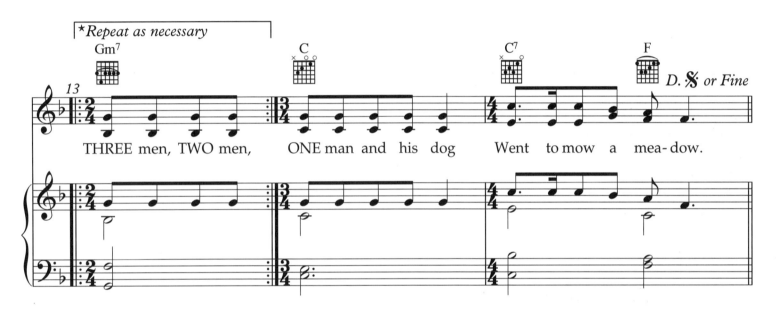

*Repeat as necessary

THREE men, TWO men, ONE man and his dog Went to mow a mea-dow.

D. % or Fine

2. TWO men went to mow,
   Went to mow a meadow.
   TWO men, ONE man and his dog
   Went to mow a meadow.

3. THREE men went to mow,
   Went to mow a meadow.
   THREE men, TWO men,
   ONE man and his dog
   Went to mow a meadow.

Continue to a predecided number of verses.

*Time signatures will alternate between ⅔ and ¾

36. The Fox

Traditional
Arr. Barrie Carson Turner

1. The fox went out on a chil - ly night, Prayed to the moon for to give him light, For he'd ma - ny a mile to go that night Be - fore he reached the town - o, town - o, town - o. He'd ma - ny a mile to

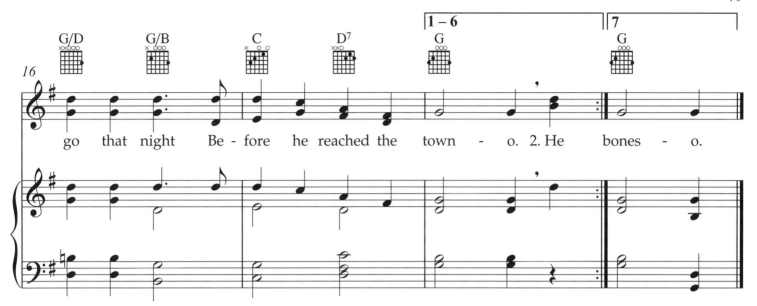

go that night   Be - fore   he reached the   town - o. 2. He   bones - o.

2. He ran till he came to a great big pen
   Where the ducks and geese were kept therein.
   'A couple of you will grease my chin
    Before I leave this town-o, town-o, town-o.
   A couple of you will grease my chin
   Before I leave this town-o'.

3. He grabbed the grey goose by the neck,
   Threw a duck across his back.
   He didn't mind the quack, quack, quack,
   And the legs all dangling down-o...

4. The farmer's wife jumped out of bed,
   Out of the window she cocked her head,
   Saying, 'John, John, the goose is gone,
   And the fox is on the town-o...'

5. Then John he ran to the top of the hill,
   Blew his horn both loud and shrill,
   The fox he said, 'I'd better flee with my kill
   For they'll soon be on my trail-o...'

6. Fox ran till he came to his cosy den,
   There were the little ones – eight, nine, ten,
   Saying, 'Daddy, you'd better go back again
   'Cause it must be a mighty fine town-o...'

7. The fox and his wife without any strife
   Cut up the goose with a carving knife.
   They never had such a supper in their life,
   And the little ones chewed on the bones-o...

37. Yankee Doodle

Traditional
Arr. Barrie Carson Turner

Yan - kee Doo - dle, Keep it up, Yan - kee Doo - dle Dan - dy, Mind the mu - sic

and the step, And with the girls be han - dy. han - dy.

2. Pa and I went down to camp
   Along with Captain Goodwin.
   There we saw the men and boys
   As thick as hasty pudding.

   Yankee Doodle, keep it up,
   Yankee Doodle Dandy,
   Mind the music and the step,
   And with the girls be handy.

3. There was Captain Washington
   Upon a slapping stallion,
   Giving orders to his men,
   I guess there was a million.

hasty pudding – *a porridge-like dish made from ground maize or corn*

38. Lavender's Blue

Traditional
Arr. Barrie Carson Turner

1. Lav - en - der's blue, dil - ly, dil - ly, lav - en - der's green.

When I am king, dil - ly, dil - ly, you shall be queen.

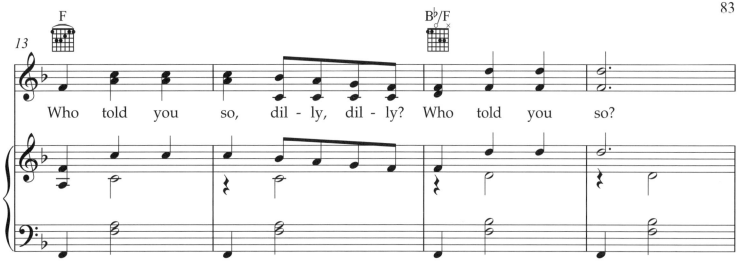

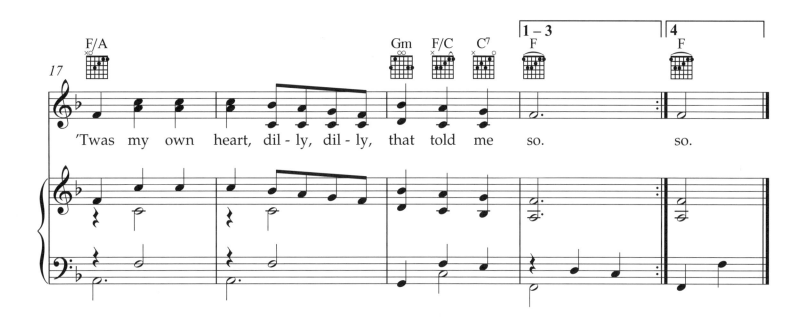

2. Call up your men, dilly, dilly, set them to work,
Some with a rake, dilly, dilly, some with a fork.
Some to make hay, dilly, dilly, some to cut corn,
While you and I, dilly, dilly, keep ourselves warm.

3. Roses are red, dilly, dilly, violets are blue,
If you love me, dilly, dilly, I will love you.
Let the birds sing, dilly, dilly, and the lambs play.
We shall be safe, dilly, dilly, out of harm's way.

4. I love to dance, dilly, dilly, I love to sing.
When I am queen, dilly, dilly, you'll be my king.
Who told me so, dilly, dilly? Who told me so?
I told myself, dilly, dilly, I told me so.

39. Kum Ba Yah

Traditional
Arr. Barrie Carson Turner

2. Someone's singing, Lord, kum ba yah.
   Someone's singing, Lord, kum ba yah.
   Someone's singing, Lord, kum ba yah.
   O Lord, kum ba yah.

3. Someone's dancing, Lord, kum ba yah...

4. Someone's weeping, Lord, kum ba yah...

5. Someone's shouting, Lord, kum ba yah...

6. Someone's praying, Lord, kum ba yah...

kum ba yah – *come by here*

40. The Old Grey Mare

Traditional
Arr. Barrie Carson Turner

Ma - ny long years a - go. Oh, the old grey mare she

ain't what she used to be. Ma - ny long years a - go. 2. Oh, the - go.

2. Oh, the small white hen don't lay like she used to lay,
   Lay like she used to lay, lay like she used to lay.
   The small white hen don't lay like she used to lay
   Many long years ago.
   Many long years ago,
   Many long years ago.
   Oh, the small white hen don't lay like she used to lay
   Many long years ago.

3. Oh, the big brown cow's gone dry – never was like this...

4. Oh, my poor black cat just sits by the fireside...

S&Co.8193 Printed in Germany

Index

A Froggy Went A-Courting	10
Aiken Drum	4
Aunt Rhody	40
Bill Groggin's Goat	42
Clementine	44
Click Go the Shears	6
Daddy Wouldn't Buy Me a Bow-Wow	69
Daisy Bell	46
Do Your Ears Hang Low?	64
Donkey Riding	8
Down in Demerara	50
I Had a Little Nut Tree	28
I Had a Rooster	72
If You're Happy and You Know It	12
Kum Ba Yah	84
Lavender's Blue	82
London Bridge is Falling Down	14
Michael Finnigan	16
Michael, Row the Boat Ashore	36
Oh, Susanna	18
Old King Cole	74
Old MacDonald Had a Farm	20
One Man Went to Mow	76
One More River	22
One, Two, Three, Four, Five	24
She'll Be Coming Round the Mountain	38
Sing a Song of Sixpence	26
Skip to My Lou	52
Ten Green Bottles	54
Ten in the Bed	30
The Bear Went Over the Mountain	66
The Fox	78
The Grand Old Duke of York	56
The Green Grass Grew All Round	60
The Old Grey Mare	86
The Tailor and the Mouse	62
There's a Big Ship Sailing	32
There's a Hole in My Bucket	58
This Old Man	34
Yankee Doodle	80